SPATIAL JUSTICE

Spatial Justice: The Basics offers a concise and accessible introduction to spatial justice as both a theoretical framework and a practical agenda for urban transformation. It examines how urban space is produced, contested, and governed, and how it is implicated in broader dynamics of inequality, recognition, and participation. Drawing on key thinkers such as Henri Lefebvre, Nancy Fraser, Iris Marion Young, Edward Soja, and Susan Fainstein, the book articulates spatial justice through its distributive, procedural, and recognitional dimensions, while also tracing its intellectual genealogy across critical theory, planning thought, and Southern urbanism.

The book centres spatial planning as a normative, political, and ethical practice capable of fostering solidarity, democratising decision-making, and addressing structural injustices. Real-world examples from Indonesia, Colombia, Brazil, the US, and more illustrate how spatial justice is negotiated in practice, while discussions of neoliberal governance, democratic backsliding, and epistemic justice ground the analysis in urgent global challenges.

Designed for upper-level undergraduates, postgraduates, and early-career professionals in planning, geography, architecture, and related fields, the book includes a detailed glossary of key terms, visual diagrams, and analytical tables to support critical engagement and classroom use.

Roberto Rocco is an associate professor of spatial planning and strategy at the Faculty of Architecture and the Built Environment at TU Delft. His research focuses on the governance of the built environment, including its formal and informal dimensions, as well as the governance of sustainability transitions, with particular emphasis on spatial justice as a core dimension of these transitions.

THE BASICS

The Basics is a highly successful series of accessible guidebooks which provide an overview of the fundamental principles of a subject area in a jargon-free and undaunting format.

Intended for students approaching a subject for the first time, the books both introduce the essentials of a subject and provide an ideal springboard for further study. With over 50 titles spanning subjects from artificial intelligence (AI) to women's studies, *The Basics* are an ideal starting point for students seeking to understand a subject area.

Each text comes with recommendations for further study and gradually introduces the complexities and nuances within a subject.

SPATIAL JUSTICE
Roberto Rocco

SPOKEN ENGLISH
Michael McCarthy and Steve Walsh

SPORT HISTORY
Gerald R. Gems

SPORT MANAGEMENT
Rob Wilson and Mark Piekarz

SPORTS COACHING
Laura Purdy

SUSTAINABILITY (SECOND EDITION)
Peter Jacques

TRANSLATION (SECOND EDITION)
Juliane House

TRANSNATIONAL LITERATURE
Paul Jay

TOWN PLANNING
Tony Hall

WOMEN'S STUDIES (SECOND EDITION)
Bonnie G. Smith

WORLD PREHISTORY
Brian M. Fagan and Nadia Durrani

For more information about this series, please visit: www.routledge.com/The-Basics/book-series/B

SPATIAL JUSTICE
THE BASICS

Roberto Rocco

NEW YORK AND LONDON

Designed cover image: Roberto Rocco

First published 2026
by Routledge
605 Third Avenue, New York, NY 10158

and by Routledge
4 Park Square, Milton Park, Abingdon, Oxon, OX14 4RN

Routledge is an imprint of the Taylor & Francis Group, an informa business

© 2026 Roberto Rocco

The right of Roberto Rocco to be identified as author of this work has been asserted in accordance with sections 77 and 78 of the Copyright, Designs and Patents Act 1988.

All rights reserved. No part of this book may be reprinted or reproduced or utilised in any form or by any electronic, mechanical, or other means, now known or hereafter invented, including photocopying and recording, or in any information storage or retrieval system, without permission in writing from the publishers.

Trademark notice: Product or corporate names may be trademarks or registered trademarks, and are used only for identification and explanation without intent to infringe.

ISBN: 978-1-041-07978-1 (hbk)
ISBN: 978-1-041-07543-1 (pbk)
ISBN: 978-1-003-64312-8 (ebk)

DOI: 10.4324/9781003643128

Typeset in Bembo
by Apex CoVantage, LLC

I dedicate this book to all those who have not surrendered to cynicism or pessimism, but who continue to imagine, demand, and work for more just, inclusive, and humane cities.

To the activists, planners, scholars, and everyday citizens who resist resignation and instead embrace hope as a political practice, solidarity as a method, and justice as a horizon. This work is for you.

To my mother, my sister, and my nephew.

CONTENTS

	About the Author	ix
	List of Figures	xi
	List of Boxes	xiii
	List of Tables	xv
	List of Acronyms	xvii
	Acknowledgements	xxi
	Preface	xxiii
1	Introduction: A Tale of Space and Injustice	1
	1.1 The Spatial Turn in the Social Sciences	14
2	Why Justice?	29
	2.1 Juridical Versus Moral Justice	32
	2.2 Justice and Science	36
	2.3 Divine Law and Natural Law	40
	2.4 Justice as Fairness	49
	2.5 Positive and Negative Rights	53
	2.6 Justice as Substantive Freedom and True Autonomy	57
3	Justice and Urban Space: Urban Space as a Site of Dispute and Cooperation	68
	3.1 Justice and Freedom in the City	70
	3.2 Agonistic Thinking	76
	3.3 A Marxist Perspective of Urban Struggles and Spatial Justice	79
	3.4 A Neoliberal Perspective	83
	3.5 Critical Theory Perspectives	86

3.6 Decolonial, Black, Indigenous, Feminist, and Queer Perspectives on Justice ... 88
  3.7 Climate Justice and Environmental Justice ... 95
  3.8 Towards a Critical and Pluriversal Approach to Justice ... 98

4 Justice and Spatial Planning ... 110
  4.1 Justice as an Internal Necessary Good in Planning and the Virtue of Planners ... 124
  4.2 Insurgent Ethics: Planning Justice Within and Against the System ... 132
  4.3 Ethical Planning Beyond the Individual ... 138
  4.4 Alternatives for Action ... 141
  4.5 Justice We Can Attain ... 143
  4.6 Schools of Thought on Justice in Planning ... 152

5 Mapping Spatial Justice: Key Thinkers and Milestones ... 162

6 Three Dimensions of Spatial Justice ... 175
  6.1 Distributive Spatial Justice ... 176
  6.2 Procedural Spatial Justice ... 188
  6.3 Recognitional Spatial Justice ... 202
  6.4 Recognition and Nancy Fraser's Status Model ... 207
  6.5 Who Gets Recognition? ... 211

7 A Spatial Justice Framework ... 225
  7.1 An Evaluative Spatial Planning Framework ... 236
  7.2 The Spatial Justice Framework: What is it for? ... 243

8 Back to Paraisópolis: Spatial Justice in Practice ... 256

9 Conclusion: Toward the Just City ... 264

Glossary of Key Terms ... 271
References ... 305
Index ... 313

ABOUT THE AUTHOR

Roberto Rocco is an associate professor of spatial planning and strategy at the Faculty of Architecture and the Built Environment at TU Delft. Trained as both an architect and a spatial planner, he holds a master's degree in planning from the University of São Paulo and a PhD from TU Delft. His research focuses on the governance for the built environment, including its formal and informal dimensions, as well as the governance of sustainability transitions, with particular emphasis on spatial justice as a core dimension of these transitions.

He has published extensively on informal urbanisation in the Global South, with a focus on how informal institutions shape and influence planning practices at the local level. Key contributions include the co-edited books *The Routledge Handbook on Informal Urbanisation* (2019) and *Insurgent Planning Practice* (2024).

Together with Caroline Newton, he co-directs the TU Delft Centre for the Just City, an initiative advancing spatial justice in the built environment through education, research, and consultancy.

FIGURES

1.1	Favela Paraisópolis, São Paulo (2014).	3
6.1	Integrated Urban Project Comuna 1.	184
6.2	Arnstein's Ladder of Citizen Participation.	193
6.3	View of Conguillío Lake and Llaima Volcano, part of Kütralkura Geopark.	217
7.1	The spatial justice triangle, a diagram showcasing the co-constitutive nature of recognition, procedure, and distribution for spatial justice.	231
7.2	The three dimensions of spatial justice are co-constitutive and mutually reinforcing.	234

BOXES

6.1	An Experience of Distributive Spatial Justice – Medellín's Urban Transformation	183
6.2	An Experience of Procedural Spatial Justice: The Los Angeles Bus Riders Union and the Title VI Consent Decree (1996–2006)	199
6.3	An Experience of Recognitional Spatial Justice – The Cultural Landscape of the Mapuche in Chile	215

TABLES

2.1 Simplified overview of schools of justice, used here to help the reader navigate different conceptions of justice. 60
4.1 Comparative ethical frameworks in spatial planning: Deontology, consequentialism, and virtue ethics. 148
7.1 A selection of justice-oriented evaluative frameworks. 237
7.2 Suggested indicators for each of the dimensions of spatial justice suggested in the spatial justice framework. 240
7.3 How spatial justice operates as a theoretical and practical framework. 249

ACRONYMS

ACC	African Centre for Cities (Cape Town, South Africa)
BCE	Before Common Era
CAHP	Claiborne Avenue History Project (New Orleans, USA)
CIDEU	Centro Iberoamericano de Desarrollo Estratégico Urbano (Ibero-American Centre for Strategic Urban Development, Chile)
CONADI	Corporación Nacional de Desarrollo Indígena (National Corporation for Indigenous Development, Chile)
CRT	Critical Race Theory
DIAD	Diversity, Interdependence, and Authentic Dialogue (Edith Innes)
EJ	Environmental Justice
EPA	United States Environmental Protection Agency
FDI	Foreign Direct Investment
G10	G10 Favelas – Slum Summit (a coalition of Brazil's ten most economically powerful favelas)
GDP	Gross Domestic Product
GEOUSP	Publication of the Human Geography Graduate Programme (PPGH) and the Physical Geography Graduate Programme (PPGF) at the University of São Paulo
GIS	Geographic Information Systems
HDI	Human Development Index

IAAC	Institute for Advanced Architecture of Catalonia (Barcelona, Spain)
IACHR	Inter-American Commission on Human Rights
IBGE	Instituto Brasileiro de Geografia e Estatística (Institute of Geography and Statistics, Brazil)
IIED	International Institute for Environment and Development (London, UK)
IPEA	Instituto de Pesquisa Econômica Aplicada (Institute for Applied Economic Research, Brazil)
LGBTQ+	Lesbian, Gay, Bisexual, Transgender, Queer/Questioning, and others
MIT	Massachusetts Institute of Technology (Cambridge, USA)
MRF	Mary Robinson Foundation – Climate Justice (Dublin, Ireland)
NGO	Non-Governmental Organisation
NPCELS	[First] National People of Colour Environmental Leadership Summit (Washington, DC)
NPR	National Public Radio (US)
NREGA	National Rural Employment Guarantee Act (India)
OECD	Organisation for Economic Cooperation and Development
OHCHR	Office of the High Commissioner for Human Rights (United Nations)
OWW	One-World World (Escobar)
PB	Participatory Budgeting
PNAD	Pesquisa Nacional por Amostra de Domicílios (National Household Sample Survey, Brazil)
PPPs	Public-Private Partnerships
PUI	Proyectos Urbanos Integrales (Integral Urban Projects, Colombia)
SCOPUS	A bibliographic database containing abstracts and citations for academic journal articles
SDGs	Sustainable Development Goals
TFT	Training for Transformation
UCC	United Church of Christ (Commission for Racial Justice, US)
UN	United Nations

UN-Habitat	United Nations Human Settlements Programme
UNDP	United Nations Development Programme
UNESCO	United Nations Educational, Scientific and Cultural Organization
UNFCCC	United Nations Framework Convention on Climate Change
UPC	Urban Poor Consortium (India)
WCED	World Commission on Environment and Development
WRI	World Resources Institute
ZEIS	Zonas Especiais de Interesse Social (Special Zones of Social Interest, Brazil)
ZRC	Zonas de Reserva Campesina (Peasant Reserve Zones, Colombia)

ACKNOWLEDGEMENTS

This book is the product of many conversations and collaborations over the years. While I take responsibility for its shortcomings, its insights and provocations are deeply indebted to a community of thinkers, practitioners, students, and colleagues who have challenged, inspired, and supported me at and around the Centre for the Just City at Delft University of Technology (TU Delft).

I am particularly indebted to Caroline Newton, Juliana Gonçalves (to whom I owe the centrality of recognitional justice in my understanding of spatial justice), Hugo Lopez, Irene Luque Martin, Johnathan Subendran, and Russell Smith (Winston-Salem State University), among others.

I thank my students at TU Delft, AMS, the Summer School *Planning and Design for the Just City*, and beyond, whose critical questions and lived experiences continue to shape how I understand spatial justice. Your insistence on making planning more ethical, inclusive, and democratic gave this book its urgency.

I owe a great intellectual debt to the scholars whose work underpins these pages. The writings of Henri Lefebvre, Iris Marion Young, Nancy Fraser, Doreen Massey, David Harvey, Ananya Roy, AbdouMaliq Simone, and Raquel Rolnik, among many others, have opened conceptual pathways and intellectual possibilities. I also thank Professor Faranak Miraftab, whose work inspires me like no other. These scholars remind us to be suspicious of 'neutrality' and to be attuned to the geographies of power, voice, and recognition. Luz Maria D'Alençon Vergara, Luisa Sotomayor, Sergio Vieda Martinez and Luciana Royer have generously reviewed parts of this manuscript.

Special thanks to my colleagues in the Section of Spatial Planning and Strategy at TU Delft, especially my biggest supporter, Remon Rooij, whose feedback, generosity, and advice made my time at TU Delft more coherent and less lonely.

I am especially grateful to those who encouraged this project from its earliest stages and offered insights on early drafts.

PREFACE

This book addresses the urgent question of how justice and injustice intersect with the spatial arrangements that organise our lives, showing how the ways we produce, govern, and inhabit space are inseparable from issues of democracy, citizenship, and social justice. It explores spatial justice as a lived and contested dimension of societal life, tracing its philosophical foundations, theoretical genealogy, and practical applications. Across its chapters, the book builds a framework grounded in distributive, procedural, and recognitional dimensions of justice, applies it to real cases, and reflects on spatial planning's role in confronting exclusionary logics and fostering more democratic futures.

As I complete this book, I find myself walking through the streets of São Paulo on a bright winter's day. The war in Ukraine rages on, the destruction of Gaza dominates the headlines, and US President Donald Trump wages a new mercantilist offensive built on punitive tariffs, rearranging global relations.

Around me, fellow citizens gather in support of Jair Bolsonaro, Brazil's far-right former president, now facing charges for plotting to subvert democratic rule. The demonstrators are easy to spot. Wearing yellow and green, the national colours of Brazil, they represent a cross-section of society, though the elderly predominate: Workers, housewives, students, secretaries, taxi drivers, and engineers. What should be a civic mobilisation has become, instead, a rally in favour of authoritarianism. It is deeply unsettling to witness such public fervour channelled into a cause so evidently harmful to the very people marching for it.

While much has been written about democratic backsliding and the global resurgence of authoritarianism, these analyses often overlook the deeper affective and material dimensions of political disillusionment and how these issues are anchored in the built environment. If we are to meaningfully confront the authoritarian turn, we must attend to the disappointment many citizens feel toward liberal democracy's failure to deliver the material and symbolic goods, both private and public, that make meaningful citizenship possible.

In its most virulent neoliberal form, late capitalism systematically deprives people of the conditions necessary to experience belonging, dignity, and agency, leaving them overworked, exhausted, and disillusioned about the future. These conditions are inseparable from the built environment and the ways it is produced, organised, and governed.

Access to dignified and healthy housing, reliable and affordable transportation, high-quality public and green spaces, and the spatial distribution and accessibility of work, education, and leisure opportunities are fundamental. Equally important are the opportunities to participate in processes of collective stewardship of resources and spaces, which foster social bonds, mutual recognition, and a shared sense of ownership over the city. When these spatial foundations are eroded or commodified, the material and symbolic bases for democratic life are weakened, making communities more susceptible to exclusionary politics and authoritarian narratives.

The political far-right has become increasingly ideological, conspiratorial, and mendacious, while much of the left has resigned itself to administering capitalism with a human face, ameliorating its worst excesses but rarely challenging its underlying logics.

It is in this context that spatial justice emerges not merely as a normative ideal, but as a transformative political project, one that confronts the structural conditions of inequality and exclusion embedded in the built environment, challenges the commodification of space, and reclaims planning as a tool for democratic co-production, recognition, and collective emancipation.

While I try to avoid excessively emotional rhetoric in academic writing, as I am aware that such language tends to obscure the strength of argumentation, there are moments when clarity demands urgency. This is one of them.

It is no overstatement to say that our collective survival depends on justice. Justice is the condition *sine qua non* for society's endurance. Without justice, understood in its structural, procedural, and recognitional dimensions, democracy becomes hollow, reduced to procedural formalities devoid of substantive popular sovereignty, prone to being hijacked by modern-day fascism.

And without true democracy, we are left defenceless against the compounded threats of authoritarianism, unrestrained capital accumulation, growing inequality, and ecological collapse. The interlocking crises of our age are not merely political, economic, or environmental failures. They are profound moral failures.

As thinkers such as Nancy Fraser, Amartya Sen, and Iris Marion Young have argued, justice must be understood both as a normative foundation for institutional design and as a lived reality that enables human flourishing and meaningful civic participation. A vibrant civic life helps anchor society in practices of reciprocity, mutual recognition, and collective responsibility; practices that resist authoritarian capture and uphold the conditions necessary for freedom and equality.

This book emerges from a place of profound sadness at the state of our world, but also from a hopeful commitment to justice as an enduring, collective pursuit. It is dedicated to those who, in diverse contexts and often against great odds, continue to struggle for a more just world.

INTRODUCTION
A Tale of Space and Injustice

In 1994, the municipality of São Paulo in Brazil proposed yet another plan to remove thousands of citizens from Favela Paraisópolis, one of the biggest slums in the city, to make way for a new avenue (Alessi, 2009; FMP, 2014; Werneck, 2018). This was not breaking news for the inhabitants of Paraisópolis. With a long history of illegal land occupation and resistance, the inhabitants of Paraisópolis were all too familiar with attempts to evict them. Another unsuccessful attempt had been made in the 1980s (IHU, 2019), and others would follow throughout the 2000s.

The favela sits on old farmland that was subdivided into plots and sold in 1921, but never properly developed because of its rugged topography. Empty lots started to be illegally occupied in the 1950s (City of São Paulo, 2009). As millions of destitute rural migrants from the impoverished Brazilian Northeast arrived in São Paulo in search of better lives, they were met with indifference by the authorities, who did next to nothing to ease the mounting housing and services crisis. Without help from the authorities and unable to afford rent or access credit, citizens took matters into their own hands and 'helped themselves' (hence the somewhat tautological expression 'self-help urbanisation') (Souza & Barifouse, 2019). By occupying public or marginal land, or negotiating with swindlers, these citizens secured small plots on which to build precarious but vital dwellings.

As the city grew, so did Paraisópolis until it became one of the largest slums in São Paulo, with over 58,500 residents crammed into approximately 118 hectares (IBGE, 2024). Despite harsh conditions, the community is situated on valuable land in one of the city's most exclusive areas. It has long been viewed as an 'eyesore' and a source of social unrest and criminality by its wealthy neighbours and city authorities (see Figure 1.1). The 1992 eviction attempt was just one more instance in the community's long history of resistance.

Using Paraisópolis' story, let's explore the broader issues of how space and social justice intersect. Paraisópolis' story extends far beyond a mere unsuccessful attempt to raze a deprived neighbourhood to the ground by building infrastructure through it, as Baron Haussmann had done in Paris in the 19th century (Willsher, 2016), a formula repeated many times over by both authoritarian and 'democratic' governments. Similar strategies have appeared in the forced clearance of Black neighbourhoods in the United States during the mid-20th century to make way for highways, such as the destruction of the Claiborne Avenue corridor in New Orleans (CAHP, no date; Gershon, 2021); the clearance of Sophiatown in apartheid-era Johannesburg to enforce racial segregation (Hart & Pirie, 1984; Lodge, 1981), and the large-scale displacements in Beijing before the 2008 Olympics to build sports infrastructure and 'beautify' the city (Human Rights Watch, 2010; Shin & Li, 2013). In each case, spatial transformation was justified under the banner of progress or order but resulted in deepened inequalities and lasting dispossession. In *The Color of Law: A Forgotten History of How Our Government Segregated America*, Richard Rothstein (2017) explains how federal, state, and local policies, including highway construction, destroyed many Black neighbourhoods and entrenched racial segregation in the United States. In *The Roots of Urban Renaissance*, Brian Goldstein (2023) also deals directly with freeway projects cutting through Black communities in that country.

These examples illustrate how the socio-economic dynamics of inclusion and exclusion are deeply entangled with space at multiple scales. This reflects what Edward Soja (2009) calls the ontological spatiality of social life: The understanding, developed from Heidegger (1962) existential analysis of *being-in-the-world* and later expanded by Casey (1997), that all social and material processes are inherently spatial. In the context of urban development, this means that policies, infrastructure projects, and planning decisions do not merely

Figure 1.1 Favela Paraisópolis, São Paulo (2014).
Source: Photo by the author.

take place in space. They actively produce and reshape spatial relations, often reinforcing patterns of inequality and exclusion.

In the case of Paraisópolis, the illegal occupation of land both facilitated the creation of place-based social and economic networks essential for the reproduction of life and, at the same time, entrenched residents' exclusion by denying them legal recognition. This paradox allowed poor rural immigrants to remain in the city and gradually reclaim their rights, even as their status as 'illegal' settlers was used to justify their marginalisation (Ballegooijen & Rocco, 2013). In this sense, the slum is the spatial expression of the idea of invented spaces of citizenship as defined by Faranak Miraftab (2004), and her central concept of insurgent planning, the idea that marginalised communities, often excluded from formal planning processes, enact their own modes of urban transformation through practices rooted in resistance, collective mobilisation, and alternative knowledge systems, which we discuss in detail later in this book.

This happened despite the continuous threat of eviction and the lack of support by the authorities, which often viewed the community as an eyesore, a den of criminality, and an obstacle to urban development rather than as a legitimate part of the city's social fabric. This often translates into invisibility. In earlier maps of the area, the community was not visible, and the area appeared as green unoccupied space. By not acknowledging the existence of the community, the authorities avoided having to provide essential services and infrastructure, which are material signs of recognition. Here, it becomes clear that recognition of the community's very existence, its history, trajectory, rights, and needs lie at the heart of the matter. We will return to the question of recognition later.

Instead of succumbing to the pressures of eviction, state violence, and lack of basic infrastructure, the residents of Paraisópolis forged resilient, self-sustaining networks that not only met their immediate needs but also laid the foundation for collective empowerment. These networks enabled them to assert their presence in the city and contest their marginalisation, showcasing urban space as a dynamic arena where struggles for justice and inclusion unfold. The community's ability to thrive in the face of systemic neglect underscores the critical role of space in shaping and being shaped by socio-political and economic realities.

It is important to highlight that the 'community' in Paraisópolis is an amalgamation of diverse groups and interests, not always conscious of the theoretical significance of their struggle. Theirs was an eminently practical endeavour: To remain in place, to work, and to earn an income. Recognising this helps avoid any romanticisation of the hardships endured by Paraisópolis's inhabitants. While many residents may be unmoved by the rhetoric of class struggle and unaware of the broader political implications of their actions, it is clear that community leadership, sometimes politically astute, not always disinterested, often opportunistic and strategic, has played a decisive role in shaping the settlement's trajectory. The space they first occupied and then transformed was an active force in their struggle, shaping and being shaped by the ways they survived, organised, and negotiated with the authorities. Borrowing from Walter Mignolo (2011), the residents of Paraisópolis were profoundly 'disobedient' in the face of an imposed socio-economic and spatial order. Yet, such disobedience required a concrete, material base from which to leverage their claims and sustain their struggle.

The point I want to make here is rather simple. Everything occurs somewhere. Even when processes happen in the mind, that mind belongs to someone located somewhere, both physically and historically. Even the immaterial flows of finance and information require spatial infrastructures to function and have spatial outcomes. In this sense, space is not only the 'place where things happen,' but an active and constitutive dimension of those happenings: A set of physically bound material, social, and symbolic relations that both enable and constrain action, shape meanings, and embed events within specific trajectories. It is simultaneously the medium, outcome, and stake of social processes, inflecting their possibilities and consequences across scales.

Paraisópolis doesn't exist in a vacuum. It sits within one of the most expensive neighbourhoods in São Paulo, adjacent to the city's new 'corporate axis' (Fix, 2007; Whitaker-Ferreira, 2000), a globally networked cluster of gleaming towers housing banks, shopping centres, and multinational headquarters. Many of these structures are held as collateral in transnational investment portfolios, their exchange value eclipsing any ongoing use or social function. Yet, this new corporate axis and the rich residential neighbourhoods around it offer inhabitants of Paraisópolis an array of low-skilled jobs in construction, cleaning, maintenance, security, food preparation, and other auxiliary services that sustain the daily operations of high-end office life (Moura, 2017). These forms of employment, while providing income, tend to reproduce structural dependency and socio-spatial hierarchies, as they are typically low-wage, insecure, and disconnected from upward mobility (Lloyd-Evans, 2008).

Financial transactions, though seemingly abstract and instantaneous, are deeply rooted in and affect specific geographic locations, illustrated by the 'Global City' paradigm of the turn of the century (Sassen, 1991, 2002). Decisions made in the stock exchanges of New York or London can trigger economic movements in cities and regions worldwide, influencing everything from employment rates, investment priorities, to urban development outcomes. The global circulation of capital often leads to investment in certain areas while divesting from others, exacerbating spatial inequalities and shaping the physical landscape through processes such as gentrification, the creation of financial districts, the emergence of special investment zones and deindustrialisation of formerly industrialised regions.

Financialisation refers to the growing predominance of transnational financial markets, institutions, and actors in shaping economic, political, social, and spatial processes (Bonizzi, 2013; French et al., 2011; Hasenberger, 2024; Lavinas et al., 2022). It marks a structural shift from economies centred on industrial production to those increasingly driven by financial logic, where investment practices, risk speculation, and asset-based income generation become central to capital accumulation. A key dimension of this process is the transformation of real estate into financial assets through practices such as mortgage securitisation, which allow residential and commercial properties to be traded in global financial markets (Aalbers, 2019; Aalbers & Gibb, 2014; Harvey, 2006). The commodification and abstraction of land and housing often lead to property price inflation, reduced affordability, and the displacement of lower-income populations in gentrifying neighbourhoods or large urban projects, particularly in cities that are integrated into global capital circuits.

David Harvey (1985) argues that urban space plays a central role in the process of capital accumulation, functioning as a *spatial fix* for surplus capital through mechanisms such as real estate speculation, infrastructure investment, and the commodification of land and housing. He demonstrates how capitalist urbanisation restructures the built environment to absorb capital, often resulting in the displacement and exclusion of marginalised populations. This process reinforces socio-spatial inequalities by privileging exchange value and profit over use value, social equity, and spatial justice. In the context of financialisation, real estate markets increasingly target high-end developments, intensifying processes of gentrification, and contributing to speculative bubbles in urban housing. The 2008 global financial crisis was emblematic of these dynamics, as it was fuelled by speculative lending practices and the treatment of housing primarily as a financial asset rather than a basic social need (Holt, 2009).

Urban space is inherently limited and socially produced, making it a site of contestation where competing claims over access, use, control, and representation frequently come into conflict. Smith and Floyd (2013) highlight how these tensions are embedded within broader political-economic structures, drawing on the 'urban growth machine' thesis developed by Molotch (1976). This framework reveals how coalitions of land-based elites, such as property developers, business interests, and municipal authorities, promote urban development strategies that prioritise exchange value, often to the detriment of local communities' needs and rights.

The growth machine thesis posits that the primary driver of urban politics, economic policy, and governance is the pursuit of growth, especially in contexts like the United States, where land and property are predominantly treated as private commodities rather than collective resources. Growth coalitions advocate for zoning changes, infrastructural investments, and public subsidies that enhance land values and attract capital, thereby maximising returns on investment in real estate. These coalitions often exert influence through lobbying and campaign financing, shaping policy outcomes in their favour.

In contrast, oppositional groups, such as neighbourhood associations, environmental advocates, and social movements, mobilise around the defence of use value. They call for policies that support public goods such as affordable housing, education, healthcare, parks, and environmental sustainability. The enduring tension between *market value* and *use value* continues to shape the urban landscape across diverse contexts, contributing to uneven development, spatial exclusion, and contested forms of urban governance. In many contemporary cities, this conflict has intensified, reaching levels that pose significant challenges to social cohesion and democratic accountability.

The inhabitants of Paraisópolis inadvertently find themselves caught up in the middle of these contested spatial dynamics, where the pressures of growth, urban redevelopment, and profit collide with their right to occupy and shape their lived environment. As their community occupies highly valuable land initially without land property titles, they have faced constant threats of eviction and exclusion, highlighting the profound inequalities embedded in urban development processes that privilege profit over the social and spatial rights of marginalised populations. Their struggle underscores the critical need for spatial justice, where equitable access, fair treatment, and recognition of their contributions to urban life are prioritised.

In view of these seemingly irreconcilable tensions, I want to return to a fundamental question posed by Doreen Massey: 'How are we going to live together?' (Massey, 2011). This deceptively simple question captures the ethical and political dimensions of urban spatial organisation. It forces us to confront the deep inequalities and power relations embedded in the ways space is shaped, used, and governed, including the tension between market value and use value. Massey's relational understanding of space, as the outcome of multiple trajectories, interactions, and social practices, reminds us that how we inhabit, share, and manage space is never neutral. It reflects broader struggles over justice, inclusion, and one's right to shape the city.

Spatial planning and land regulation play a crucial role in mediating these tensions, but their focus and application often differ according to societal models and governance frameworks. In market-driven systems, such as liberal democracies where neoliberal governance prevails, spatial planning frequently prioritises economic growth, favouring exchange value through policies that attract investment, stimulate real estate markets, and encourage urban expansion. This approach often exacerbates inequalities by marginalising communities that cannot compete within these market-oriented frameworks. It is not a fair fight.

Conversely, in models that emphasise collective welfare, spatial planning is more likely to align with the principles of use value. Here, regulations focus on ensuring equitable access to resources, protecting public spaces, creating and maintaining public goods, and safeguarding the rights of marginalised populations. For example, inclusionary zoning, rent controls, and the preservation of affordable housing are tools that prioritise social objectives over market imperatives, reflecting a commitment to spatial justice.

Massey's question, 'How are we going to live together?' encapsulates a profound ontological and political challenge. Her relational understanding of space calls upon planners, policymakers, and citizens to engage in deliberative, inclusive processes capable of holding together multiple, and often conflicting, trajectories, histories, and aspirations. To do so, spatial governance must move beyond technocratic allocation and assessment, embracing instead a pluriversal approach grounded in the recognition that space is constituted through diverse worldviews, relational ontologies, and place-based knowledges. In this book, I aim to explore how such an approach can be advanced through prefigurative practices, which, though not fully pluriversal, offer pathways toward more inclusive and just spatial futures.

Achieving spatial justice under such a framework requires the simultaneous pursuit of three interrelated goals: Redressing historical and structural unfair or unjust spatial patterns of distribution (distributive justice), enabling meaningful participation and co-decision in spatial development to both empower vulnerable communities and to access their unique knowledges and ways of being (procedural justice), and finally, affirming the situated knowledge, trajectories and identities of diverse communities (recognitional justice). This entails addressing enduring spatial inequities and injustices and institutionalising governance mechanisms that allow marginalised voices to actively participate in shaping urban and rural transformations.

At its core, Massey's perspective calls for a critical interrogation of the tension between exchange value and use value in the production of space. From this standpoint, spatial justice demands that space not be governed primarily as a site of efficiency, commodification, or competitive advantage, but rather as a material and symbolic domain for fostering human capabilities, ecological sustainability, social solidarity, and practices of care. The just organisation of spatial resources, how they are distributed, governed, and imbued with meaning, reveals much about a society's ethical and political orientation. In particular, recognising the differentiated spatial and historical trajectories and lived experiences of diverse social groups becomes central to advancing a more inclusive and just spatial order. The idea of trajectories is central to Massey's relational ontology of space. Here, space is continually made and remade through the interweaving trajectories of people, places, and power. The notion of trajectories implies continuous movement and change. It is inherently multiple, always under construction, and shaped by both material conditions and discursive practices. This perspective resists essentialism and determinism, instead emphasising contingency, heterogeneity, and the ongoing negotiation of difference. Massey's relational space demands an ethics of responsibility, as spatial configurations reflect and reproduce broader socio-political inequalities and possibilities for transformation.

In this sense, Massey's relational ontology does more than describe space, it offers a normative and analytical lens for exposing how spatial arrangements shape, and are shaped by, broader socio-political struggles. It invites us to conceptualise space as an always-contested terrain where justice is neither fixed nor abstract, but must be continuously negotiated through democratic, plural, and future-oriented practices.

In addressing this question, the concept of spatial justice emerges as a central concern. It challenges us to ensure that competing claims over space, whether between social groups, economic interests, or environmental needs, are resolved in ways that are equitable, inclusive, and sustainable. This entails recognising urban space as both a social product and a public good, a collective *oeuvre* in the words of Lefebvre, requiring frameworks that balance individual freedoms with collective values and responsibilities. Ultimately, the resolution of these spatial conflicts not only shapes the physical and social landscapes of our communities but also defines the conditions for coexistence, equity, and justice in an interconnected and interdependent world.

But why justice? What makes it a distinct yet pivotal human institution? My simple answer is that it is essential to answer Massey's question. We can only live together in peace and flourish in societies when we achieve some form of justice. As John Rawls asserts in his monumental book *A Theory of Justice* (1971), justice is 'the first virtue of social institutions,' meaning that it provides the normative foundation upon which all other societal arrangements must be evaluated. Without justice, institutional arrangements lose legitimacy, no matter how efficient or well-organised they may appear. In this book, we will see how an idea of perfect justice might not be helpful, particularly because, as Amartya Sen (2009) argues, the pursuit of justice is not about constructing an ideal, fully just society, but about identifying and removing clear injustices in the world we inhabit, making the world more just today than it was yesterday. Justice, in this sense, becomes not a static end state, but a dynamic and ongoing practice of public reasoning, negotiation, and societal reform.

In the next section of the Introduction, I examine the 'spatial turn' in the social sciences to show why space is not merely a passive 'stage' upon which the social and economic are enacted, but an ontologically constitutive dimension of socio-economic and political relationships. This ontological turn is key to understanding how space actively shapes and is shaped by power relations, cultural and political practices, and economic structures, making it central to diagnosing and transforming conditions of spatial justice. This ontological turn also means that spatial justice must be conceived not only in terms of equitable outcomes but also as an ongoing process of reconfiguring the spatial relations, institutions, and imaginaries that enable or constrain the realisation of justice in practice.

Chapter 2, Why Justice? establishes justice as the ethical and political foundation of life in society, grounded in fairness, dignity, and the dismantling of oppressive structures. It distinguishes juridical justice (legality) from moral justice (right outcomes and processes), stressing that legality does not always guarantee justice. Justice is presented as both culturally and historically contingent and anchored in enduring principles, tracing its evolution from divine and natural law traditions to modern democratic ideals of the *res publica*. The chapter engages with major philosophical contributions: John Rawls's *Justice as Fairness*, Amartya Sen's capability approach, Nancy Fraser's multidimensional theory, and Iris Marion Young's focus on recognition and participation, linking these to public reasoning, contestation, and institutional design. Justice is positioned as a plural, dynamic, and contested practice shaped by values, ethics, and cultural understandings. Crucially, it frames justice as a form of praxis requiring active public engagement and political struggle, not merely legal compliance or technocratic design. By situating justice at the centre of spatial governance, this chapter lays the normative base for later discussions of planning's distributive, procedural, and recognitional dimensions, showing why spatial arrangements and governance processes must be evaluated against principles of justice.

Chapter 3, Justice and Urban Space, conceptualises the city as a dynamic and contested arena in which justice is shaped through the constant interplay of power, conflict, and cooperation. Drawing on Doreen Massey, it understands space as relational, historically layered, and open to multiple trajectories. The chapter explores enduring tensions between freedom and justice, tracing their philosophical roots and connecting them to contemporary urban dilemmas. Incorporating Chantal Mouffe's agonistic pluralism, it argues that democratic life in the city requires engaging with, rather than suppressing, conflict. It examines how Marxist, neoliberal, and Critical Theory perspectives reveal the reproduction of spatial inequalities through capitalist accumulation, market logics, and ideology, while decolonial, Black, Indigenous, feminist, and queer approaches expose epistemic violence and advance alternative spatial ontologies. Finally, the chapter links environmental and climate justice to spatial justice, emphasising the need for equitable socio-spatial arrangements across scales and temporalities. This chapter establishes the theoretical breadth of the book by situating spatial justice within diverse philosophical, political, and critical traditions, showing how justice in the city is shaped by, and must respond to, conflict, power, and difference.

Chapter 4, Justice and Spatial Planning, positions spatial planning as both a potential instrument of spatial justice and a mechanism of exclusion, depending on how it addresses distributive, procedural, and recognitional concerns. It traces the discipline's historical entanglement with state power, technocracy, and market logics, showing how it has often reproduced structural injustices. The chapter argues for reorienting planning toward democratic, redistributive, and recognitional goals, drawing on critical, communicative, and radical planning traditions. Central to this reorientation is the concept of *insurgent ethics*, an ethical and political stance for planners grounded in solidarity, moral courage, and alignment with grassroots struggles against exclusionary spatial orders. This ethic extends beyond individual virtue to demand structural and institutional transformation, creating conditions for meaningful participation, redistribution of resources, and recognition of diverse ways of knowing and living. Recognising planners as political actors embedded in power relations, the chapter calls for working both in and against the capitalist state to democratise decision-making and redistribute power. Linking insurgent ethics to Nancy Fraser's participatory parity and Chantal Mouffe's agonistic democracy, it frames planning as a site of contestation where conflict can be harnessed as a driver of justice rather than suppressed. This chapter defines planning's role in the book by framing it as a political arena where ethical practice, institutional reform, and productive engagement with conflict are essential to advancing spatial justice.

Chapter 5, Mapping Spatial Justice: Key Thinkers and Milestones, traces the intellectual roots of spatial justice, linking earlier normative debates to the thinkers and movements that shaped its contemporary form. It moves from Lefebvre's production of space and right to the city, through territorial justice, to radical geography's critiques of technocratic distributional models. Key figures – Harvey, Massey, Fraser, Young – expand its distributive, procedural, and recognitional dimensions, while Southern perspectives from Holston, Miraftab, Roy, and Simone challenge Eurocentric frameworks and centre marginalised epistemologies. Susan Fainstein's *Just City* operationalises justice in planning through equity, democracy, and diversity, bridging theory and practice. Soja popularises 'spatial justice' as an analytical category, and Marcuse reinforces systemic critiques of capitalism's spatial logics. Postcolonial and Southern urbanist voices extend the scope to informality, infrastructure, climate justice, and de-coloniality. By mapping this diverse genealogy, the chapter situates spatial justice as a contested but fertile field, preparing the ground for Chapter 6.

Chapter 6, Three Dimensions of Spatial Justice, elaborates distributive, procedural, and recognitional justice as interdependent dimensions of spatial justice. It defines each dimension, traces theoretical roots in thinkers such as Fraser, Young, and Harvey, and demonstrates their interplay in shaping equitable urban outcomes. By connecting material allocation, decision-making processes, and cultural recognition, it offers a robust conceptual model for diagnosing injustice and guiding planning practice. Functionally, this chapter anchors the book's analytical framework, preparing readers for its operationalisation in Chapter 7.

Chapter 7, **A Spatial Justice Framework**, operationalises the distributive, procedural, and recognitional dimensions by integrating them with five conceptual functions – normative, prescriptive, descriptive, explanatory, and analytical. It offers a flexible evaluative tool for diagnosing injustice, guiding interventions, and fostering transformative change in planning. Drawing on Fraser, Young, Lefebvre, and others, it stresses the co-constitutive nature of justice dimensions and warns against spatial fetishism. The framework bridges theory and practice, enabling context-sensitive, historically grounded, and participatory approaches to urban equity.

Chapter 8, Back to Paraisópolis: Spatial Justice in Practice, applies the book's spatial justice framework to the lived realities of São Paulo's second-largest favela. Functionally, it grounds the theoretical model in an empirical case, demonstrating how distributive, procedural, and recognitional injustices converge and how residents contest them. Historical resistance to eviction, economic embeddedness, and strategic location underpin its collective agency. The case illustrates how space can simultaneously reproduce inequality and enable insurgent citizenship, offering a nuanced, situated understanding of spatial justice.

The concluding chapter, **Chapter 9**, consolidates the book's core argument that spatial justice is the ethical and political foundation of planning. The chapter calls for moving beyond individual virtue ethics toward institutional reform, deep democracy, and ontological plurality. The just city is framed as a horizon, never fully attainable but continuously pursued through collective action, care, and resistance, anchoring spatial justice as both vision and method.

We now turn to the ontological foundations of spatial justice, beginning with the intellectual shifts that redefined space as a constitutive dimension of social life.

1.1 THE SPATIAL TURN IN THE SOCIAL SCIENCES

At the heart of this new understanding of space as central to social processes is the 'spatial turn' in the social sciences. This intellectual movement began in the late 20th century, emphasising the significance of space, place, and geography in understanding social phenomena (Bachmann-Medick, 2016; Santos, 2021a). Scholars across various disciplines, led by Henri Lefebvre, building upon Heidegger and others, later joined by names such as Peter Marcuse, Edward Soja, David Harvey, and Susan Fainstein, recognised that spatial dimensions are not merely passive backgrounds for social action but active elements that shape social relationships, power dynamics, and cultural practices. This movement shifted focus from temporal and political analyses to considering how spatial arrangements influence political, economic, and social structures. It underscored the importance of space as a critical factor in the production and reproduction of societal processes, leading to new insights into topics like globalisation, the connection between capital and urbanisation, and environmental issues.

Historically, space was treated as absolute or geometric. Early human geography and sociology used spatial analysis descriptively, focusing on environmental determinism (Meyer, 2020) and regional geography.

The early to mid-20th century saw the emergence of functional and economic perspectives, with Walter Christaller's *Central Place Theory* (Christaller & Baskin, 1966), originally published in 1933, and Alfred Weber's theories of industrial location, which treated space in quantitative and functional terms, aligning with positivist approaches (Weber & Friedrich, 2021).

Martin Heidegger made a profound contribution to the theory of space, particularly through his existential and phenomenological philosophy. Heidegger challenged traditional notions of space as an abstract, measurable container, proposing instead that space is inherently relational and tied to human existence, particularly in his *Being and Time* (1962), originally published in 1927. For Heidegger, space is not something 'out there' but is constituted by our lived experience, our being-in-the-world (*Dasein*). He argued that space emerges through the relationships and interactions between people, objects, and their environment, and that these interactions are imbued with meaning. Heidegger's concept of *dwelling* emphasises how humans experience and shape space as part of their everyday existence, situating spatiality at the core of human being. This understanding of space as relational and dynamic influenced subsequent thinkers, including Henri Lefebvre, who expanded these ideas to explore the social production of space. Heidegger's work laid the philosophical groundwork for the spatial turn, encouraging scholars to examine how space is actively created and re-created through human practices and experiences, rather than being a fixed or neutral backdrop.

During the 1960s and 1970s, Marxist critiques and the concept of social production of space gained greater prominence. Marxist geographers challenged functionalist and positivist approaches, emphasising the economic and political processes shaping spatial arrangements. David Harvey's *Social Justice and the City* (1973) reframes urban space as a site of class struggle and capital accumulation. Henri Lefebvre's *The Right to the City* (1968) and *The Production of Space* (1974) argued that space is socially produced, embedding power dynamics, ideologies, and material practices. Lefebvre's conceptual triad, perceived, conceived, and lived space, became foundational for spatial theory.

The 1980s and 1990s saw the emergence of postmodern and feminist influences. Postmodern geographers critiqued grand narratives and stressed the plurality of spatial experiences. Edward Soja, in *Postmodern Geographies* (1989) and *Thirdspace* (1996), built on Lefebvre's ideas, introducing the 'trialectics of space,' real (physical), imagined (conceptual), and lived (experiential), as a framework for understanding spatial justice.

We have explored Massey's feminist geography in the previous section, emphasising the relational and fluid nature of space. As we have seen, Massey, in works like *For Space* (Massey, 2005), argued that space is dynamic, constructed by intersecting trajectories, and inherently political. We will return to Massey's ideas several times in this book.

Contemporarily, the spatial turn in the social sciences has seen as interdisciplinary expansion. The spatial turn has influenced a wide array of disciplines, from anthropology to sociology, emphasising how space intersects with race, gender, class, and identity. Michel Foucault's exploration of spatial power in *Discipline and Punish* (1975) and his concept of heterotopias further connected geography to political theory. Most importantly, the Global South has contributed to decolonise the discourse, with authors like Ananya Roy and Faranak Miraftab exploring informality and insurgent planning, highlighting spatial justice in postcolonial contexts.

Henri Lefebvre is perhaps the intellectual 'founder' of the spatial turn, building on Heidegger, Hegel, Marx, Nietzsche, and others. Heidegger's existential phenomenology, especially his concepts of 'being-in-the-world' and the ontological centrality of spatiality, influenced Lefebvre's understanding of space as dynamic and central to human experience. However, Lefebvre's approach diverges from Heidegger's metaphysical focus, grounding spatial analysis in materialist and Marxist analysis.

According to Schmid (2012), Lefebvre's work incorporates three distinct elements that form the foundation of his innovative theory of space production. Lefebvre developed a unique version of dialectical thinking that diverged from traditional binary frameworks. His approach is *triadic*, drawing on Hegel, Marx, and Nietzsche. It encompasses *perceived space* (physical and material realities), *conceived space* (mental constructs and representations), and *lived space* (encompassing experiential, emotional, and symbolic aspects). This triadic framework allows for a more comprehensive understanding of space as both a product and a producer of social relations. It transcends rigid dualisms by emphasising the interplay between material conditions, ideological constructs, and everyday lived experiences in shaping spatial realities.

This original perspective, often misunderstood, is central to his philosophical contributions and offers a more nuanced and dynamic understanding of social processes. Lefebvre crafted his own theory of language, heavily influenced by Nietzsche, which, according to Schmid, has been largely overlooked in discussions of his work, even amidst the linguistic turn in social sciences. Through this lens, Lefebvre applied his triadic dialectic to concrete phenomena, emphasising the active and interpretive nature of language in shaping social realities.

According to Serpa (2014), while Heidegger's influence on Lefebvre has been extensively discussed in literature, the contributions of French phenomenologists Maurice Merleau-Ponty and Gaston Bachelard to his work remain underexplored. These thinkers informed Lefebvre's engagement with lived experience and the materiality of space, enriching his theoretical framework.

Lefebvre's *Le Droit à la ville* (*The Right to the City*), first published in 1968 (Lefebvre, 1968), significantly influenced the spatial turn in the social sciences and later discussions on spatial justice. The book argues for the centrality of urban space in the lives of individuals and communities, advocating for a transformative approach to urbanisation that prioritises human needs and participation in urban life, much like the ancient Greeks conceived of citizenship.

Lefebvre's work was pivotal in the spatial turn for several reasons. *Le Droit à la ville* introduced a critical perspective on how urban space is produced and managed. This critique influenced subsequent spatial analyses across disciplines, encouraging scholars to consider the spatial dimensions of social phenomena.

Lefebvre's work transcended disciplinary boundaries, drawing on philosophy, sociology, geography, and urban studies to articulate his vision of urban space. This interdisciplinary approach contributed to the spatial turn by demonstrating the relevance of spatial analysis across the social sciences. His advocacy for the active participation of urban residents in the creation and transformation of their spaces through the idea of the right to the city was crucial to later urban social movements.

In *Le Droit à la ville*, Lefebvre famously stated, '*Le droit à la ville est un cri et une demande*' (the right to the city is both a cry and a demand). This powerful statement encapsulates the essence of Lefebvre's argument for a radical reimagining of urban life and planning, where citizens are central to the processes of creating and shaping their living environments. Lefebvre's assertion frames the right to the city as an active demand for greater participation and influence in the urban development process. It emphasises the need for residents to have not only access to urban spaces but also a decisive role in how spaces are designed, used, and managed. By characterising the right to the city as a 'cry,' Lefebvre highlights the insurgent nature of the right to the city and the urgent need to address the exclusion and marginalisation experienced by many urban residents. It underscores the disparities in how urban spaces are allocated and who benefits from urban development, advocating for a more equitable distribution of urban resources. The notion of the right to the city as a 'demand' asserts the agency of urban dwellers. It challenges top-down, technocratic approaches to urban planning, proposing instead that cities should be shaped by the collective desires, needs, and creativity of their inhabitants.

The year 1968 was marked by widespread escalation of social movements across the globe, from the May student protests in Paris, which rapidly escalated to national protests in France and student protests in Mexico, Argentina, Brazil, Poland, the US, Czechoslovakia, Germany, and more, to the Civil Rights Movement in the United States, the beginning of the Troubles in Ireland, the Tlatelolco massacre in Mexico City, and an escalation of the guerilla against the military dictatorship in Brazil. That year was also marked by widespread protests against the Vietnam War in the context of the Cold War. These movements were driven by a demand for greater social justice, anti-war sentiment, and a yearning for more civil rights. The drive of 1968 underscored the inadequacies of existing social and political structures and highlighted the global interconnectedness of social injustices. Lefebvre's work recognised the protagonism of urban spaces as the places for collective empowerment and the enactment of public demands, reinforcing the idea that justice must encompass not only political and economic dimensions but also the spatial organisation of society.

In *La production de l'espace* (*The Production of Space* (1974)), Lefebvre reinterprets space not just as a lived phenomenon (a focus in Heidegger) but also as a socially produced entity shaped by historical, economic, and political forces. While Heidegger emphasised individual and existential experiences of space, Lefebvre incorporated collective, systemic, and structural dimensions, informed by Marxist thought. He reinterprets space not just as a lived phenomenon, but also as a socially produced entity shaped by greater historical, economic, and political forces.

Lefebvre critiques Heidegger for lacking a concrete historical and material analysis of space. Heidegger's focus on the ontological and metaphysical dimensions of being did not engage with how space is shaped by capitalism, power dynamics, or class struggle, key concerns in Lefebvre's work derived from Marxist thought. This practical and material orientation sets him apart from Heidegger's more abstract and philosophical discussions of being and space.

According to Schmid (2012), Nietzsche's contribution to Henri Lefebvre's triadic conception of space lies in his emphasis on individual experience, creativity, and the dynamic, ever-changing nature of existence. Lefebvre drew from Nietzsche's critique of rigid structures and static metaphysics to emphasise lived space, the experiential and symbolic dimension of space that reflects emotions, imagination, and human subjectivity. Nietzsche's influence is evident in Lefebvre's rejection of purely mechanistic or deterministic views of social processes. Instead, Nietzsche's celebration of individual agency, will to power, and the importance of interpretation informs Lefebvre's idea that lived space is where resistance, reinvention, and cultural meaning emerge. Nietzsche's critique of hierarchical truths and dominant ideologies resonates with Lefebvre's insistence on viewing space as contested and continuously produced through human interaction and conflict.

This focus on the creative and existential aspects of human life, drawn from Nietzsche, complements Lefebvre's incorporation of Heidegger's phenomenology (emphasising the embodied and situated experience of being), Hegelian dialectics (focused on totality), and Marxist materialism (focused on social structures). Together, they form a triadic framework that integrates material, mental, and lived dimensions, making Lefebvre's theory of space dynamic, inclusive, and open-ended. This synthesis underscores Lefebvre's ability to bridge structural forces, individual agency, and existential experience, offering a holistic understanding of the production and experience of space. In summary, Lefebvre illustrated a shift in the social sciences that caters for the 'ontological spatiality of all being' (Iveson, 2011, p. 253), as already mentioned, the fundamental idea that physical space is inherent to the existence and experiences of all entities and phenomena.

In *Social Justice and the City* (1973), David Harvey critically examines the spatial dimensions of social justice, interrogating how resources, opportunities, and burdens are distributed across urban environments. In the first part of the book, Harvey works within a liberal framework, introducing the notion of territorial social justice, the idea that justice can be assessed by examining spatial distributions of goods and services relative to need. However, he soon expresses dissatisfaction with this approach, ultimately adopting a more radical, Marxist perspective that foregrounds the structural production of injustice through capitalist urbanisation (Pirie, 1983). This shift marks Harvey's departure from distributive models of justice toward a historical-materialist critique of the socio-economic structures that produce spatial inequality.

Harvey's conceptual foundations draw from Marxist political economy, dialectical materialism, and Henri Lefebvre's theory of the production of space. Together, these frameworks enable a deeper understanding of how urban space is not merely the site where injustice occurs, but an active medium through which capital accumulation is pursued, class power is exercised, and inequalities are reproduced. By linking spatial injustice to the internal contradictions of capital, Harvey recasts justice not as a moral ideal but as a question of political economy, inseparable from the logic of accumulation, dispossession, and uneven development.

His work has been pivotal in reorienting debates on urban justice toward a dynamic understanding of how space and society are co-constitutive. Rather than treating justice as a static, abstract principle, Harvey urges us to analyse the underlying processes, economic, political, and spatial, that give rise to inequality and exclusion. This perspective continues to shape contemporary debates in urban studies, particularly on gentrification, displacement, and the financialisation of housing.

While Harvey later moved beyond the specific language of territorial social justice, the concept nonetheless adds an important layer to understanding urban inequality. His early observations on how cities concentrate diversity, density, and interdependence highlight the need to balance individual freedoms with collective needs, a tension that makes justice in the city inherently spatial, relational, and contested. In this context, freedom is never absolute but always exercised in relation to others, requiring constant negotiation. Justice, therefore, is not only a normative aspiration but a spatial and political condition shaped by the urban fabric itself.

Milton Santos contributed to the foundations of a spatial ontology since the 1970s, particularly in works such as *Por Uma Geografia Nova* (2021b), originally published in 1978 and *Espaço e Sociedade* (1979). Across these writings, he began dismantling the notion of space as a Cartesian category, an abstract, absolute dimension divorced from the social processes that produce and transform it.

Instead, he framed it as a social product, shaped by the interplay between material forms (the 'technical' dimension) and the social processes (the 'social' dimension) that inhabit and transform them.

In *The Nature of Space* (Santos, 2021a), originally published in 1996, he consolidated this new ontology of space in relation to social phenomena, conceptualising space as a dynamic, inseparable synthesis of material form, social processes, and temporal change.

Rejecting both purely physicalist and purely social abstractions, Santos defines space as a system of *objects* (natural and human-made) and *actions* (social practices, flows, and uses), whose interrelations are historically situated and constantly transformed. In this view, space is a concrete totality where the technical, political, and economic dimensions converge, and where the interplay between fixed structures and dynamic flows shapes social life. By embedding space within the logic of social reproduction, Santos advances an ontology that links the physical arrangements of the built environment to the evolving strategies of capital, the state, and everyday actors. His framework insists that spatial forms embody and reproduce power relations, yet are also the terrain of resistance and transformation. This relational and processual understanding situates spatial justice within broader struggles over the control, meaning, and use of space, making *The Nature of Space* a crucial reference for rethinking the ontological status of space in social theory.

Across Henri Lefebvre, Doreen Massey, David Harvey, and Milton Santos, we get a process-relational ontology of space: Space is produced (not given), relational, and open, historically constituted through power-laden practices, and unevenly structured by capitalist political economy. Lefebvre argues that space is actively produced through social relations and everyday practices, conceived, perceived, and lived (Lefebvre, 1974). This undercuts any view of space as a neutral container. Massey insists space is a 'simultaneity of stories-so-far': Relational, dynamic, and always under construction rather than a closed surface (Massey, 2005). This helps avoid teleology and spatial determinism. Harvey shows how capitalist accumulation, fixes, and spatial-temporal strategies (e.g. 'accumulation by dispossession') continuously remake geographies and entrench uneven development (Harvey, 1973, 1985, 1997, 2012).

Santos foregrounds the 'technical-scientific-informational milieu,' the 'used territory,' and the dual circuits of the urban economy, illuminating how peripheral formations and everyday infrastructures co-produce space under globalisation (Santos, 1979, 2021a, 2021b).

Taken together, these claims cohere into a new spatial ontology ('new' relative to older absolute or substantival notions): Space is a contingent, multi-scalar assemblage of relations, institutions, infrastructures, and representations, continually produced and contested. It is neither purely discursive nor purely material; it is a sociomaterial process saturated by power and difference (Harvey, 2006; Lefebvre, 1974; Massey, 2005; Santos, 2021a). In sum, it is both a place where socio-economic processes unfold and an active force in shaping those processes, structuring possibilities, constraints, and meanings, while also providing the material and symbolic terrain on which these relations can be resisted, reworked, and transformed.

This position has consequences for a normative grounding for spatial justice in subsequent chapters of this book. If space is produced, justice concerns the *processes* and *relations* that make geographies: Distributional outcomes, procedures of decision-making, and recognition of plural subjects are all spatially constituted.

Planning is part of the production of space. Hence, planning interventions should reshape *relations* (rules, rights, infrastructures, representations) rather than merely allocate *things*. This reframes planning from site design to institution building and infrastructural justice (Lefebvre, 1974; Santos, 1996. This relocation of planning will be discussed in depth in Chapter 2.

Again, planning is part of the production of space, playing a larger or smaller role according to its capacity to shape the material, institutional, and symbolic dimensions of urban life. Where planning operates with strong regulatory authority, extensive financial resources, and institutional legitimacy, it can decisively steer spatial trajectories: Zoning codes, infrastructure investments, and public space design not only allocate resources but actively constitute the relations, flows, and identities that give space its form and meaning (Lefebvre, 1974; Harvey, 2006). In contexts where planning is institutionally weak, underfunded, or politically marginalised, such as in many cities of the Global South or neoliberal regimes dominated by market logics, its contribution to the production of space may be indirect, fragmented, or subordinated to private or informal actors (Miraftab, 2009; Roy, 2009).

Its degree of influence also depends on the scalar and temporal reach of planning interventions. Strategic, long-term metropolitan frameworks can reconfigure entire regional economies and ecologies over decades, while small-scale neighbourhood plans might only modulate existing dynamics without significantly altering the broader socio-spatial order. Crucially, the planning system's embeddedness in power relations, whether it functions as an agent of market facilitation, state control, grassroots empowerment, or hybrid governance, determines the type of space it helps to produce. This reinforces the need to analyse planning not as a neutral technical instrument, but as a socio-political practice that can either reproduce or contest existing patterns of spatial injustice.

From this perspective, the planner's agency is obviously far from stabilised. It is mediated by political will, institutional arrangements, civic engagement, and the presence of counter-forces in civil society. Yet, even when constrained, planning participates in the ongoing production of space, sometimes in overt, large-scale transformations, other times in subtle regulatory shifts, representational framings, or the selective mobilisation of knowledge. Recognising this variability is essential for situating planning within the relational ontology of space advanced in this book, and for understanding why interventions must be assessed not only by their immediate physical outputs but by their role in shaping the socio-spatial processes through which justice or injustice takes form.

From an epistemic stance, this ontology pushes us to hold multiple temporalities and geographies at once, combining Northern theory with Southern insights about everyday economies, informalities, and peripheries, so justice claims are simultaneously provincialised and (re)connected to larger circuits (Santos, 1979, 1996).

If space is continually produced through the interplay of social relations, political decisions, market forces, and material infrastructures, then the question inevitably arises: *Produced for what, for whom, and to whose benefit?* The relational ontology outlined in this chapter reveals that spatial configurations are never merely technical artefacts: They embody particular values, political path dependencies, ideologies, and priorities, resulting in different distributions of resources, opportunities, and recognition, privileging some trajectories while constraining others. This recognition forces us to confront the normative dimension of spatial production: Once we accept that space could be otherwise, we must also ask what ought to guide its remaking. It is here that the question of justice becomes unavoidable. Justice offers the ethical and political compass by which to evaluate not only the outcomes of spatial arrangements but also the processes and relations through which they are produced. Chapter 2, therefore, turns to an introductory account of the intellectual and philosophical foundations of justice, tracing its historical formulations and contemporary debates, in order to establish the normative ground on which a theory and practice of spatial justice can stand.

REFERENCES

Aalbers, M. B. (2019). Financial geography III: The financialization of the city. *Progress in Human Geography*, *44*(3). https://doi.org/10.1177/030913251985

Aalbers, M. B., & Gibb, K. (2014). Housing and the right to the city: Introduction to the special issue. *International Journal of Housing Policy*, *14*(3), 207–213. https://doi.org/10.1080/14616718.2014.936179

Alessi, N. A. (2009). *Formam-se Favelas e Ganham Importância no Cenário Urbano São Paulo: Heliópolis e Paraisópolis*. University of São Paulo. https://www.teses.usp.br/teses/disponiveis/8/8136/tde-24042009–150118/publico/NELSON_ANTONIO_ALESSI_corrig_rec_16_04_09.pdf

Bachmann-Medick, D. (2016). *The cultural turns: New orientations in the study of culture*. Walter de Gruyter.

Ballegooijen, J. v., & Rocco, R. (2013). The ideologies of informality: Informal urbanization in the architectural and planning discourses. *Third World Quarterly*, *34*(10), 1794–1810.

Bonizzi, B. (2013). Financialization in developing and emerging countries: A survey. *International Journal of Political Economy*, *42*(4), 83–107. https://www.jstor.org/stable/24696310

CAHP. (no date). *Why is the Claiborne avenue history project important?* CAHP. Retrieved August 10, 2025, from https://claiborneavenue.wordpress.com/why-is-the-claiborne-avenue-history-project-important/

Casey, E. S. (1997). *The fate of place: A philosophical history*. University of California Press.

Christaller, W., & Baskin, C. W. (1966). *Central places in southern Germany*. Prentice-Hall.

City of São Paulo. (2009). *Como Surgiu Paraisópolis*. Prefeitura de São Paulo. Retrieved August 16, 2025, from https://prefeitura.sp.gov.br/web/habitacao/paraisopolisold/historia

Fix, M. (2007). *São Paulo Cidade global: Fundamentos Financeiros de uma Miragem*. Boitempo/ANPUR.

FMP. (2014). *Fórum Multientidades de Paraisópolis*. FMP. Retrieved August 15, 2025, from, https://multientidades.virtual.org.br/wp-content/uploads/Linha-do-tempo-forum-multientidades_r1.pdf?utm

Foucault, M. (1975). *Discipline and punish: The birth of the prison*. Random House.

French, S., Leyshon, A., & Wainwright, T. (2011). Financializing space, spacing financialization. *Progress in Human Geography*, *35*(6), 798–819. https://doi.org/10.1177/0309132510396749

Gershon, L. (2021). *The highway that sparked the demise of an iconic Black Street in New Orleans*. Smithsonian Magazine. Retrieved August 10, 2025, from https://www.smithsonianmag.com/smart-news/documenting-history-iconic-new-orleans-street-and-looking-its-future-180977854/?utm

Goldstein, B. D. (2023). *The roots of urban renaissance: Gentrification and the struggle over Harlem*. Princeton University Press.

Hart, D. M., & Pirie, G. H. (1984). The sight and soul of Sophiatown. *Geographical Review*, 74(1), 38–47. https://doi.org/10.2307/214759

Harvey, D. (1973). *Social justice and the city*. University of Georgia Press. https://www.jstor.org/stable/j.ctt46nm9v

Harvey, D. (1985). *The urbanization of capital: Studies in the history and theory of capitalist urbanization 2*. Blackwell.

Harvey, D. (1997). *Justice, nature and the geography of difference*. Wiley-Blackwell. https://www.wiley.com/en-us/Justice%2C+Nature+and+the+Geography+of+Difference-p-9781557866813

Harvey, D. (2006). *The limits to capital*. Verso.

Harvey, D. (2012). *Rebel cities: From the right to the city to the urban revolution*. Verso.

Hasenberger, H. (2024). What is local government financialisation? Four empirical channels to clarify the roles of local government. *Urban Studies*, 61(11), 2039–2059. https://doi.org/10.1177/00420980231222133

Heidegger, M. (1962). *Being and time*. Blackwell.

Holt, J. (2009). A summary of the primary causes of the housing bubble and the resulting credit crisis: A non-technical paper. *The Journal of Business Inquiry*, 8(1), 120–129. https://journals.uvu.edu/index.php/jbi/article/view/211

Human Rights Watch. (2010). *China: Beijing relocations put migrants at risk*. Human Rights Watch. Retrieved August 10, 2025, from https://www.hrw.org/news/2010/03/31/china-beijing-relocations-put-migrants-risk?utm

IBGE. (2024). *2022 Census: 16.4 million persons in Brazil lived in Favelas and urban communities*. Agência IBGE Notícias. Retrieved August 15, 2025, from https://agenciadenoticias.ibge.gov.br/en/agencia-news/2184-news-agency/news/41813-2022-census-16-4-million-persons-in-brazil-lived-in-favelas-and-urban-communities?utm

IHU. (2019). *Paraisópolis, a história de uma comunidade sitiada*. Outras Mídias. Retrieved August 16, 2025, from https://outraspalavras.net/outrasmidias/paraisopolis-a-historia-de-uma-comunidade-sitiada/?utm

Iveson, K. (2011). Social or spatial justice? Marcuse and Soja on the right to the city. *City*, 15(2), 250–259. https://doi.org/10.1080/13604813.2011.568723

Lavinas, L., Bressan, L., Rubin, P., & Cordilha, A. C. (2022). *The financialisation of social policy: An overview* [UFRJ-IE, Discussion Paper 001/2022]. https://www.ie.ufrj.br/images/IE/TDS/2022/TD_IE_001.pdf

Lefebvre, H. (1968). *Le Droit à la ville*. Anthropos.

Lefebvre, H. (1974). La production de l'espace. *L'Homme et la société. Sociologie de la connaissance marxisme et anthropologie.*, 31–32, 15–32.

Lloyd-Evans, S. (2008). Geographies of the contemporary informal sector in the Global South: Gender, employment relationships and social protection. *Geography Compass*, 2(6), 1885–1906. https://doi.org/10.1111/j.1749-8198.2008.00157.x

Lodge, T. (1981). The destruction of Sophiatown. *The Journal of Modern African Studies*, *19*(1), 107–132. http://www.jstor.org/stable/160608

Massey, D. (2005). *For space*. Sage.

Massey, D. (2011). *Spatial justice: Radical spatial foundations*. Centre for the Study of Democracy', University of Westminster and the 'Westminster International Law & Theory Center' and the Spaces of Democracy/Democracy of Space Network'. Retrieved September 15, from https://www.youtube.com/watch?v=kFIpcfl4pEA

Meyer, W. B. (2020). Environmental determinism. In A. Kobayashi (Ed.), *International encyclopedia of human geography* (pp. 175–181). Elsevier. https://doi.org/10.1016/B978-0-08-102295-5.10743-7.

Mignolo, W. D. (2011). Epistemic disobedience and the decolonial option: A manifesto. *Trans Modernity*, *1*(2). https://doi.org/10.5070/T412011807

Miraftab, F. (2004). Invited and invented spaces of participation: Neoliberal citizenship and feminists' expanded notion of politics. *Wagadu*, *1*(1–7), 89–101. https://doi.org/10.1177/0739456X04267173

Miraftab, F. (2009). Insurgent planning: Situating radical planning in the Global South. *Planning Theory*, *8*(1), 32–50. https://doi.org/10.1177/1473095208099297

Molotch, H. (1976). The city as a growth machine: Toward a political economy of place. *American Journal of Sociology*, *82*(2), 309–332. https://doi.org/10.1086/226311

Moura, P. M. d. (2017). *Paraisópolis: 74% dos moradores com emprego fixo trabalham no Morumbi* Veja. Retrieved August 14, 2025, from https://vejasp.abril.com.br/cidades/paraisopolis-morumbi/

Pirie, G. H. (1983). On spatial justice. *Environment and Planning A*, *15*(1), 465–473. https://doi.org/10.1068/a150465

Rawls, J. (1971). *A theory of justice*. Harvard University Press.

Rothstein, R. (2017). *The colour of law: A forgotten history of how our government segregated America*. Liveright.

Roy, A. (2009). Why India cannot plan its cities: Informality, insurgence and the idiom of urbanization. *Planning Theory*, *8*(1), 76–87. https://www.jstor.org/stable/26165886

Santos, M. (1979). *Espaço e Sociedade*. Editora Vozes.

Santos, M. (1996). *A natureza do espaço – técnica e tempo: Razão e emoção*. Hucitec.

Santos, M. (2021a). *The nature of space*. Duke University Press. https://lccn.loc.gov/2021000786

Santos, M. (2021b). *Por uma geografia nova: Da crítica da geografia a uma geografia crítica*. EDUSP.

Sassen, S. (1991). *The global city: New York, London, Tokyo*. Princeton University Press.

Sassen, S. (2002). Locating cities on global circuits. *Environment & Urbanization*, *14*(1), 13–30. https://doi.org/10.1177/095624780201400102

Schmid, C. (2012). A teoria da produção do espaço de Henri Lefèbvre: Em direção a uma dialética tridimensional. *GEOUSP*, *32*(1), 89–109. https://doi.org/10.11606/issn.2179-0892.geousp.2012.74284

Sen, A. (2009). *The idea of justice*. Belknap Press of Harvard University Press.

Serpa, A. (2014). A Teoria das Representações em Henri Lefèbvre: Por uma abordagem cultural e multidimensional da geografia. *GEOUSP_ Espaço Tempo*, *18*(3), 487–495. https://doi.org/10.11606/issn.2179-0892.geousp.2014.83538

Shin, H. B., & Li, B. (2013). Whose games? The costs of being "Olympic citizens" in Beijing. *Environment & Urbanisation*, *25*(2), 559–576. https://doi.org/10.1177/0956247813501139

Smith, J. W., & Floyd, M. F. (2013). The urban growth machine, Central Place Theory and access to open space. *City, Culture and Society*, *4*(2), 87–98. https://doi.org/10.1016/j.ccs.2013.03.002

Soja, E. (1989). *Postmodern geographies: The reassertion of space in critical social theory*. Verso.

Soja, E. (1996). *Thirdspace: Journeys to Los Angeles and other real-and-imagined places*. Blackwell.

Soja, E. (2009). The city and spatial justice. *Justice spatiale/spatial justice*, *1* (September 2009).

Souza, F., & Barifouse, R. (2019). *Paraisópolis, 100 anos: Como loteamento de luxo virou favela mais famosa de SP, BBC Brazil*. BBC. Retrieved May 5, 2022, from https://www.bbc.com/portuguese/brasil-50694377

Weber, A., & Friedrich, C. J. (2021). *Alfred weber's theory of the location of industries*. Hassell Street Press.

Werneck, R. M. (2018). *As Percepções dos Moradores do Grotão da Favela de Paraisópolis/SP sobre o Processo de Urbanização: As Condições de Vida e o Direito à Moradia* Pontifícia Universidade Católica de São Paulo. https://sapientia.pucsp.br/bitstream/handle/21415/2/Raquel%20Machado%20Werneck.pdf?utm

Whitaker-Ferreira, J. S. (2000). Globalização e Urbanização Subdesenvolvida. *São Paulo em Perspectiva*, *14*(4), 10–20.

Willsher, K. (2016). Story of Cities #12: Haussmann rips up Paris – and divides France to this day. *The Guardian*. https://www.theguardian.com/cities/2016/mar/31/story-cities-12-paris-baron-haussmann-france-ursban-planner-napoleon